D0769509

Pre- and Re-, Mis- and Dis-

What Is a Prefix?

To Maximilian Baraka Cleary
—B.P.C.

To Carol Hinz and all the folks at Lerner
for making these wonderful books possible
—M.G.

Prefix:
A word part added to the beginning of a word or root to change its meaning

Cleary, Brian P., 1959–
Pre- and re-, mis- and
dis- : what is a prefix?
2013.
33305228644666
sa   08/12/13

Pre- and Re-, Mis- and Dis-

What Is a Prefix?

by Brian P. Cleary

illustrations by Martin Goneau

M MILLBROOK PRESS / MINNEAPOLIS

Prefixes are word parts that we add onto a word.

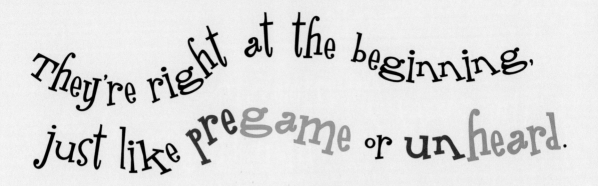

They're right at the beginning,
just like **pregame** or **unheard**.

These word parts change the meaning of the word to which they're added.

Examples might be **underclothes,**

revisit,

or unpadded.

The root words are the main words,

as in padded,

visit,

clothes.

The prefixes are letters that we see in front of those.

im– and un– and non– and il–
and dis– are some of them.

defrost, untie, misspell.

Anti- means "against," like antitheft and antifreeze.

The first part means "opposing." Are you catching on to these?

other times, a prefix
serves to give a number clue.

Like **bi**– before a root word,
Which hints to us there's two.

Binoculars have two glass lenses;

bicycles, two wheels;

bilingual folks, two languages
to tell us how they feel.

19

like preheat

and prepayment,

*Pay now!
Get it when
it ships.*

preschool, and many more.

As in retype, recalculate,

repaint,

rebuild,

resend.

like multicolor multiplex. Can you come up with any?

Trans- will sometimes mean "across."
It often hints at movement.

"He transferred to a transatlantic school and showed improvement."

So many words, it might just cause your brain to overload!

So What is a prefix? Do you know?

PREFIX	MEANING	EXAMPLE
anti-	opposite of; against	antisocial, antiwar
bi-	occurring two times	biannual
de-	away from; opposite of	depart, declutter
dis-	opposite of	dislike
em-/en-	put in or on; to cause	empower, enrage
fore-	at the front; before	forehead, forecast
il-	opposite of (used before roots beginning with l)	illegal
im-	opposite of (used before roots beginning with b, m, or p)	impolite
in-	opposite of	inexpensive
inter-	between, among	international
mis-	wrong, bad; not	misbehave, misunderstanding
multi-	many or much	multimedia
non-	not	nonstop
pre-	before	preview
pro-	forward, going ahead	proactive
over-	over; in excess	overnight, overcook
re-	to do again	rewrite
semi-	half; partly	semicircle, semidarkness
sub-	under, less than	subway, subtract
trans-	across	transport
un-	not; opposite of	unhappy; unlock
under-	under; too little	undersea, underestimate

EXTRA TERRESTRIAL

HAPPY

UN HAPPY

31

Find activities, games, and more at
www.brianpcleary.com

ABOUT THE AUTHOR AND ILLUSTRATOR

BRIAN P. CLEARY is the author of the best-selling Words Are CATegorical® series as well as the Math Is CATegorical®, Food Is CATegorical™, Animal Groups Are CATegorical™, Adventures in Memory™, and Sounds Like Reading® series. He has also written *Do You Know Dewey? Exploring the Dewey Decimal System, Six Sheep Sip Thick Shakes: And Other Tricky Tongue Twisters,* and several other books. Mr. Cleary lives in Cleveland, Ohio.

MARTIN GONEAU is the illustrator of the Food Is CATegorical™ and Animal Groups Are CATegorical™ series. Mr. Goneau lives in Trois-Rivières, Québec.

Text copyright © 2013 by Brian P. Cleary
Illustrations copyright © 2013 by Lerner Publishing Group, Inc.

All rights reserved. International copyright secured. No part of this book may be reproduced, stored in a retrieval system, or transmitted in any form or by any means—electronic, mechanical, photocopying, recording, or otherwise—without the prior written permission of Lerner Publishing Group, Inc., except for the inclusion of brief quotations in an acknowledged review.

Millbrook Press
A division of Lerner Publishing Group, Inc.
241 First Avenue North
Minneapolis, MN 55401 U.S.A.

Website address: www.lernerbooks.com

Main body text set in RandumTEMP 35/48.
Typeface provided by House Industries.

Library of Congress Cataloging-in-Publication Data

Cleary, Brian P., 1959—
    Pre- and re-, mis- and dis- : what is a prefix? / By Brian P. Cleary ; Illustrated by Martin Goneau.
        pages   cm. — (Words Are CATegorical)
    ISBN 978—0—7613—9031—2 (lib. bdg. : alk. paper)
    ISBN 978—1—4677—1712—0 (eBook)
    1. English language—Suffixes and prefixes—Juvenile literature. 2. Language arts (Primary) I. Goneau,
Martin, illustrator. II. Title.
PE1175.C54 2013
425'.92—dc23   2013001050

Manufactured in the United States of America
1 — BP — 7/15/13